MUSICAL MASTERPIECES IN POETRY

BY DR. MURRAY J. LEVITH

To the memory of my father

Published by Paganiniana Publications, Inc.
P.O. Box 427, Neptune, NJ 07753

Contents

Acknowledgments

"The Fiddler" by Thomas Hardy. From *Complete Poems* by Thomas Hardy, edited by James Gibson (New York: Macmillan, 1978).

"The Fiddler of Dooney" by William Butler Yeats. Reprinted with permission of Macmillan Publishing Co., Inc. from *Collected Poems* by William Butler Yeats. Copyright 1906 by Macmillan Publishing Co., Inc.; renewed 1934 by W. B. Yeats.

"Fiddler Jones" by Edgar Lee Masters. From *Spoon River Anthology*, Macmillan Publishing Co., Inc. Reprinted by permission of Ellen C. Masters.

"Music" by Amy Lowell. From *The Complete Poetical Works of Amy Lowell.* Copyright 1955 by Houghton Mifflin Company. Reprinted by permission of the publisher.

"The Aim Was Song" by Robert Frost. From *The Poetry of Robert Frost*, edited by Edward Connery Lathem. Copyright 1923, 1969 by Holt, Rinehart and Winston. Copyright 1951 by Robert Frost. Reprinted by permission of Holt, Rinehart and Winston, Publishers.

"Piano Practice" by Rainer Maria Rilke. From Rainer Maria Rilke, *Selected Works*, II, translated by J. B. Leishman. Copyright The Hogarth Press Ltd., 1960. Reprinted by permission of New Directions.

"Jazz Fantasia" by Carl Sandburg. From *Smoke and Steel* by Carl Sandburg, copyright 1920 by Harcourt Brace Jovanovich, Inc.; copyright 1948 by Carl Sandburg. Reprinted by permission of the publisher.

"The Flute of the Lonely" by Vachel Lindsay. From *Collected Poems* by Vachel Lindsay (New York: Macmillan, 1925).

"Piano Practice at the Academy of the Holy Angels" by Wallace Stevens. From *Opus Posthumous* by Wallace Stevens, edited by Samuel French Morse. Copyright 1957 by Elise Stevens and Holly Stevens. Reprinted by permission of Alfred A. Knopf, Inc.

"The Dance" by William Carlos Williams. From *Collected Later Poems* of William Carlos Williams. Copyright 1944 by William Carlos Williams. Reprinted by permission of New Directions.

Introduction

Poetry and music are sister arts. Each depends upon sound, rhythm, and structure, among other things, to convey its message. Both poetry and music are first composed, then performed or read. Such re-creation takes place in time. Some poetry attempts to eclipse denotative meaning and thus strains toward music and, contrarily, some music seems so programmatically literal as to tell a story.

While music is usually heard in performance and not read from the score, poetry is, to be sure, mostly seen on the page. The reader of poetry, therefore, becomes analogous to the performer of music—an interpreter. We return to those poems in our "repertoire" which we love but also, just as the musical virtuoso, we seek out challenging new works to stir us intellectually and emotionally.

This anthology of musical poems contains a sampling of fine verse, some familiar but some not so, by the very best writers. Represented is English and American poetry (with a few Continental examples) from the sixteenth century to the present, from Shakespeare and Milton to Robert Frost and Wallace Stevens. Minority writers and women poets are included.

For reasons of space, I have limited my selection to relatively short lyrics which are readily available to the reader (without footnotes) on a literal level. Much "older" poetry unfortunately requires footnotes to explain diction, usage, or allusion, and some "new" requires notes for similar reasons. Since this collection is meant primarily for musicians—interested in another kind of notes—exclusion of more esoteric verse seemed desirable. I have arranged the poetry chronologically according to the birth dates of the poets in order to give some idea of the historical sweep of the lyrics.

There are perhaps a few surprises—that Walt Whitman found "Italian Music in Dakota," that Carl Sandburg and Langston Hughes could capture so well the feeling of jazz rhythms in verse, that D. H. Lawrence wrote a musical poem. What does not surprise, however, is the consistently high quality of the poetry contained in this collection; for here are represented some of the finest practitioners of the poet's art and, indeed, some very great poems.

The illustrations were selected with considerable care and accompany most of the poems. Though they are fine images in themselves when standing alone, each was chosen as an appropriate visual picture for a given poem. Some of the illustrations enhance the word image, others the lyrical feeling, historical context, or general spirit of the poem involved. I was obliged to select pictures that would reproduce well in black and white; thus, most of the illustrations are taken from prints—etchings, engravings, woodcuts, and lithographs.

For help with this book I would like to thank Skidmore College, Dr. Eric Weller, Dean of the Faculty; the Skidmore College Library; Dr. Lynne L. Gelber, who translated Charles Baudelaire's "La Musique"; and my two student assistants, Maureen Bouley and Maureen Hille. Also, the New York Public Library, Elizabeth E. Roth, Keeper of Prints; Worcester Art Museum, The Detroit Institute of Art, National Gallery of Art; and the Hyde Collection, Glens Falls, New York, James Kettlewell, Curator. Finally, Tina, Nathaniel, and Will provide daily music and poetry for me and deserve the most thanks of all.

Murray J. Levith
Skidmore College
Saratoga Springs, New York

∽∾

Sir Thomas Wyatt
(1503-1542)

Reputed to be the lover of Anne Boleyn before she married Henry VIII, Sir Thomas Wyatt is most remembered for helping to introduce the sonnet form into English Literature. Wyatt's poetry was influenced by conventional Petrarchan love themes (such as, ill-treatment by a mistress) and the use of far-fetched metaphoric comparisons called "conceits." "Blame Not My Lute" was doubtless written to be set to music and sung with lute accompaniment.

BLAME NOT MY LUTE

Blame not my lute for he must sound
  Of this or that as liketh me;
For lack of wit the lute is bound
  To give such tunes as pleaseth me:
Though my songs be somewhat strange,
And speaks such words as touch thy change,
    Blame not my lute.

My lute, alas, doth not offend,
  Though that perforce he must agree
To sound such tunes as I intend
  To sing to them that heareth me;
Then though my songs be somewhat plain,
And toucheth some that use to feign,
    Blame not my lute.

My lute and strings may not deny,
  But as I strike they must obey;
Break not them, then, so wrongfully,
  But wreak thyself some wiser way:
And though the songs which I indite
Do quit thy change with rightful spite,
    Blame not my lute.

Spite asketh spite, and changing change,
  And falsed faith must needs be known;
The fault so great, the case so strange,
  Of right it must abroad be blown:
Then since that by thine own desert
My songs do tell how true thou art,
    Blame not my lute.

Blame but the self that hast misdone
  And well deserved to have blame;
Change thou thy way so evil begun,
  And then my lute shall sound that same:
But if till then my fingers play
By thy desert their wonted way,
    Blame not my lute.

"Lute Player" by Hans Brosamer

11

Farewell, unknown, for though thou break
   My strings in spite, with great disdain,
Yet have I found out for thy sake
   Strings for to string my lute again;
And if perchance this foolish rhyme
Do make thee blush at any time,
      Blame not my lute.

William Shakespeare
(1564-1616)

The poems and plays of William Shakespeare are filled with musical references and allusions—books have been written on the subject. "Sonnet 128" is one of two of the Bard's sonnets centrally about music (the other is "Sonnet 8"). Here the speaker of the poem addresses his lady about her skills on the virginal. He wishes aloud that he might receive as much of her favor as her instrument does.

SONNET 128

How oft, when thou, my music, music play'st
Upon that blessed wood whose motion sounds
With thy sweet fingers, when thou gently sway'st
The wiry concord that mine ear confounds,
Do I envy those jacks that nimble leap
To kiss the tender inward of thy hand
Whilst my poor lips, which should that harvest reap,
At the wood's boldness by thee blushing stand!
To be so tickled, they would change their state
And situation with those dancing chips
O'er whom thy fingers walk with gentle gait,
Making dead wood more blest than living lips.
  Since saucy jacks so happy are in this,
  Give them thy fingers, me thy lips to kiss.

"Lady Playing the Virginals" by Wenceslaus Hollar

15

Robert Herrick
(1591-1674)

Robert Herrick is generally considered the greatest Cavalier Poet of seventeenth-century England. Herrick's verse shows considerable classical influence, but it is his simple designs and care with embellishment and detail that distinguish his work. His lyrical gifts are dazzling. Herrick wrote both religious and secular poetry and, in "To Music, To Becalm His Fever," he brings together diction from both areas to make a fine statement about the powers of music.

TO MUSIC, TO BECALM HIS FEVER

Charm me asleep, and melt me so
  With thy Delicious Numbers;
That being ravished, hence I go
  Away in easy slumbers.
    Ease my sick head,
    And make my bed,
Thou Power that canst sever
    From me this ill:
    And quickly still:
    Though thou not kill
      My Fever.

Thou sweetly canst convert the same
  From a consuming fire,
Into a gentle-licking flame,
  And make it thus expire,
    Then make me weep
    My pains asleep;
And give me such reposes,
    That I, poor I,
    May think, thereby,
    I live and die
      'Mongst Roses.

Fall on me like a silent dew,
  Or like those Maiden showers,
Which, by the peep of day, do strew
  A Baptism o'er the flowers.
    Melt, melt my pains,
    With thy soft strains;
That having ease me given,
    With full delight,
    I leave this light;
    And take my flight
      For Heaven.

Courtesy of the Worcester Art Museum, Worcester Massachusetts

"Young Woman Playing a Clavichord," from the workshop of Jan Sanders van Hemessen

George Herbert
(1593-1633)

George Herbert is remembered today as the simple priest-poet from Bemerton in England. His verse is religious and personal, stressing his beliefs and many failings and, occasionally, a rebellious spirit. Herbert's posthumously published book The Temple *describes, among other things, what one encounters in and around a church. There are poems about, for example, "The Altar," "The Church Floor," "The Windows." "Church Music," reprinted here, is typical of the series.*

CHURCH MUSIC

Sweetest of sweets, I thank you! When displeasure
   Did through my body wound my mind,
You took me thence, and in your house of pleasure
   A dainty lodging me assigned.

Now I in you without a body move,
   Rising and falling with your wings.
We both together sweetly live and love,
   Yet say sometimes, "God help poor kings."

Comfort, I'll die; for if you post from me,
   Sure I shall do so, and much more.
But if I travel in your company,
   You know the way to heaven's door.

"The Organ" by Martin Engelbrecht

John Milton
(1608-1674)

John Milton's father was a fine amateur musician, and encouraged his son's musical interests from an early age. The poet could play keyboard instruments and reportedly had a pleasant singing voice. Milton's poetry is much influenced by music both in form and content. As we can observe in "At a Solemn Music," church music had a special appeal for the poet.

AT A SOLEMN MUSIC

Blest pair of Sirens, pledges of Heaven's joy,
Sphere-born harmonious sisters, Voice and Verse,
Wed your divine sounds, and mixed power employ,
Dead things with inbreathed sense able to pierce;
And to our high-raised fantasy present
That undisturbed song of pure concent,
Aye sung before the sapphire-colored throne
To him that sits thereon,
With saintly shout and solemn jubilee;
Where the bright Seraphim in burning row
Their loud uplifted angel-trumpets blow,
And the Cherubic host in thousand choirs
Touch their immortal harps of golden wires,
With those just Spirits that wear victorious palms,
Hymns devout and holy psalms,
Singing everlastingly:
That we on Earth, with undiscording voice,
May rightly answer that melodious noise;
As once we did, till disproportioned sin
Jarred against nature's chime, and with harsh din
Broke the fair music that all creatures made
To their great Lord, whose love their motion swayed
In perfect diapason, whilst they stood
In first obedience, and their state of good.
O may we soon again renew that song,
And keep in tune with Heaven, till God ere long
To his celestial consort us unite,
To live with him, and sing in endless morn of light!

Andrew Marvell
(1621-1678)

Andrew Marvell was a colleague and friend of John Milton. A brilliant lyricist, Marvell wrote fine poetry in a variety of genres: love lyrics, religious verse, a marvelous short epic, satire, and much occasional poetry. In "Music's Empire," he imagines Creation in musical terms.

MUSIC'S EMPIRE

First was the world as one great cymbal made,
Where jarring winds to infant Nature played.
All music was a solitary sound,
To hollow rocks and murmuring fountains bound.

Jubal first made the wilder notes agree;
And Jubal tuned music's first jubilee:
He called the echoes from their sullen cell,
And built the organ's city where they dwell.

Each sought a consort in that lovely place;
And virgin trebles wed the manly base.
From whence the progeny of numbers new
Into harmonious colonies withdrew.

Some to the lute, some to the viol went,
And others chose the cornet eloquent,
These practising the wind, and those the wire,
To sing men's triumphs, or in heaven's choir.

Then music, the mosaic of the air,
Did of all these a solemn noise prepare:
With which she gained the empire of the ear,
Including all between the earth and sphere.

Victorious sounds! Yet here your homage do
Unto a gentler conqueror than you:
Who though he flies the music of his praise,
Would with you heaven's hallelujahs raise.

John Dryden
(1631-1700)

John Dryden was the foremost writer of the late seventeenth century, and served for a time as England's poet laureate. He had his hand in a number of operas, including one based on Milton's Paradise Lost. St. Cecilia, *the patron saint of music whose day is celebrated on November 22, attracted Dryden's attention several times in his poetry. "A Song for St. Cecilia's Day, 1687," reprinted here, was set to music by the Italian composer Giovanni Battista Draghi.*

A SONG FOR ST. CECILIA'S DAY, 1687

From harmony, from heavenly harmony
　　This universal frame began:
　　When Nature underneath a heap
　　　Of jarring atoms lay,
　　And could not heave her head,
The tuneful voice was heard from high:
　　"Arise, ye more than dead."

Then cold, and hot, and moist and dry,
In order to their stations leap,
　　And Music's power obey.
From harmony, from heavenly harmony
　　This universal frame began:
　　From harmony to harmony
Through all the compass of the notes it ran,
The diapason closing full in Man.

What passion cannot Music raise and quell!
　　When Jubal struck the corded shell,
　　His listening brethren stood around,
　　And, wondering, on their faces fell
　　To worship that celestial sound.
Less than a god they thought there could not dwell
　　Within the hollow of that shell
　　That spoke so sweetly and so well.
What passion cannot Music raise and quell!

　　The Trumpet's loud clangor
　　　Excites us to arms,
　　With shrill notes of anger,
　　　And mortal alarms.
　　The double double double beat
　　　Of the thundering Drum
Cries: "Hark! the foes come;
Charge, charge, 'tis too late to retreat."

The soft complaining Flute
In dying notes discovers
The woes of hopeless lovers,
Whose dirge is whispered by the warbling Lute.
Sharp Violins proclaim
Their jealous pangs, and desperation,
Fury, frantic indignation,
Depth of pains, and height of passion,
For the fair, disdainful dame.

But O! what art can teach,
What human voice can reach,
The sacred Organ's praise?
Notes inspiring holy love,
Notes that wing their heavenly ways
To mend the choirs above.

Orpheus could lead the savage race;
And trees unrooted left their place,
Sequacious of the lyre;
But bright Cecilia raised the wonder higher;
When to her Organ vocal breath was given,
An angel heard, and straight appeared,
Mistaking earth for heaven.

GRAND CHORUS
As from the power of sacred lays
The spheres began to move,
And sung the great Creator's praise
To all the blest above;
So, when the last and dreadful hour
This crumbling pageant shall devour,
The Trumpet shall be heard on high,
The dead shall live, the living die,
And Music shall untune the sky.

"Saint Cecilia" by Domenichino

Samuel Johnson
(1709-1784)

The dictionary maker Samuel Johnson was one of the best conversationalists of his age. He was also a journalist, novelist, playwright, biographer, critic, and poet. Johnson once observed: "The delight which music affords seems to be one of the first attainments of rational nature; wherever there is humanity, there is modulated sound." One of his moving short lyrics remembers the Welsh violinist Claudy Phillips, who died in poverty after a career of some acclaim.

AN EPITAPH ON CLAUDY PHILLIPS,
A MUSICIAN

Phillips, whose touch harmonious could remove
The pangs of guilty pow'r, and hapless love,
Rest here distress'd by poverty no more,
Find here that calm, thou gav'st so oft before.
Sleep, undisturb'd, within this peaceful shrine,
Till angels wake thee, with a note like thine.

"Vanitas-Still Life" by Edwaert Colyer

George Gordon, Lord Byron
(1788-1824)

In many ways Byron's life epitomized romance, and his poetry was a virtual outgrowth of the fortune of his birth and his adventuresome spirit. A Lord at ten years of age, his education was the best: first tutors, then Dulwich, Harrow, and Trinity College Cambridge. He traveled extensively, dying in Greece while fighting for a cause. Some of Byron's romantic spirit can be seen in his "Stanzas for Music."

STANZAS FOR MUSIC

There be none of Beauty's daughters
  With a magic like thee;
And like music on the waters
  Is thy sweet voice to me:
When, as if its sound were causing
The charmed ocean's pausing,
The waves lie still and gleaming,
And the lulled winds seem dreaming;

And the midnight moon is weaving
  Her bright chain o'er the deep;
Whose breast is gently heaving,
  As an infant's asleep:
So the spirit bows before thee;
To listen and adore thee;
With a full but soft emotion,
Like the swell of summer's ocean.

"The Banjo Lesson" by Mary Cassatt

Percy Bysshe Shelley
(1792-1822)

Shelley exhibited the characteristic freedom of spirit that we associate with the romantic temperament. He was a rebel almost from the start—at school and in his social relationships. The last years of Shelley's brief life were spent in Italy where he wrote most of his poetry. "To Jane" captures some of the lyrical beauty for which Shelley is famous. The "Jane" of the poem was Jane Williams. Shelley bought her a guitar, and may have had an affair with her during the last year of his life.

TO JANE

The keen stars were twinkling
And the fair moon was rising among them,
        Dear Jane.
    The guitar was tinkling
But the notes were not sweet 'till you sung them
        Again.—
    As the moon's soft splendour
O'er the faint cold starlight of Heaven
        Is thrown—
    So your voice most tender
To the strings without soul had then given
        Its own.

    The stars will awaken,
Though the moon sleep a full hour later,
        Tonight;
    No leaf will be shaken
While the dews of your melody scatter
        Delight.
    Though the sound overpowers
Sing again, with your dear voice revealing
        A tone
    Of some world far from ours,
Where music and moonlight and feeling
        Are one.

Ralph Waldo Emerson
(1803-1882)

Ralph Waldo Emerson emphasized the intuitive and spiritual above the empirical, and thus came to be known as a "transcendentalist." His philosophy resulted from a unique mixture of a Unitarian background, passion for Platonic thought, and fascination with mysticism. In the poem "Music," we observe Emerson's belief in the universal "song" of nature and the cosmos.

MUSIC

Let me go where'er I will,
I hear a sky-born music still:
It sounds from all things old,
It sounds from all things young,
From all that's fair, from all that's foul,
Peals out a cheerful song.

It is not only in the rose,
It is not only in the bird,
Not only where the rainbow glows,
Nor in the song of woman heard,
But in the darkest, meanest things
There alway, alway something sings.

'T is not in the high stars alone,
Nor in the cup of budding flowers,
Nor in the redbreast's mellow tone,
Nor in the bow that smiles in showers,
But in the mud and scum of things
There alway, alway something sings.

Elizabeth Barrett Browning
(1806-1861)

Elizabeth Barrett Browning's courtship by Robert Browning and her own love story resulted in her most famous book: Sonnets From the Portuguese. *Who does not recognize the poem beginning: "How do I love thee? Let me count the ways." But Mrs. Browning wrote other poetry as well and, as we can see from "A Musical Instrument," fine poetry at that.*

A MUSICAL INSTRUMENT

What was he doing, the great god Pan,
  Down in the reeds by the river?
Spreading ruin and scattering ban,
Splashing and paddling with hoofs of a goat,
And breaking the golden lilies afloat
  With the dragon-fly on the river.

He tore out a reed, the great god Pan,
  From the deep cool bed of the river:
The limpid water turbidly ran,
And the broken lilies a-dying lay,
And the dragon-fly had fled away,
  Ere he brought it out of the river.

High on the shore sat the great god Pan,
  While turbidly flowed the river;
And hacked and hewed as a great god can,
With his hard bleak steel at the patient reed,
Till there was not a sign of a leaf indeed
  To prove it fresh from the river.

He cut it short, did the great god Pan,
  (How tall it stood in the river!)
Then drew the pith, like the heart of a man,
Steadily from the outside ring,
And notched the poor dry empty thing
  In holes, as he sat by the river.

"This is the way," laughed the great god Pan,
  (Laughed while he sat by the river,)
"The only way, since gods began
To make sweet music, they could succeed."
Then, dropping his mouth to a hole in the reed,
  He blew in power by the river.

Sweet, sweet, sweet, O Pan!
   Piercing sweet by the river!
Blinding sweet, O great god Pan!
The sun on the hill forgot to die,
And the lilies revived, and the dragon-fly
   Came back to dream on the river.

Yet half a beast is the great god Pan,
   To laugh as he sits by the river,
Making a poet out of a man:
The true gods sigh for the cost and pain,—
For the reed which grows nevermore again
   As a reed with the reeds in the river.

"Daphnis Plays to his Goats" by Aristide Maillol

Edgar Allan Poe
(1809-1849)

Fascination with the remarkable life of Edgar Allan Poe often detracts from consideration of this writer's tremendous achievements in fiction, criticism, and poetry. Indeed, Poe was a literary genius. His poetry is enormously musical, and has a characteristic tone of ominous mystery about it. No one has ever written better or more hauntingly about bells.

THE BELLS

I

Hear the sledges with the bells—
Silver bells!
What a world of merriment their melody foretells!
How they tinkle, tinkle, tinkle,
In the icy air of night!
While the stars that oversprinkle
All the heavens, seem to twinkle
With a crystalline delight;
Keeping time, time, time,
In a sort of Runic rhyme,
To the tintinnabulation that so musically wells
From the bells, bells, bells, bells,
Bells, bells, bells—
From the jingling and the tinkling of the bells.

II

Hear the mellow wedding bells
　　　　Golden bells!
What a world of happiness their harmony foretells!
　　　Through the balmy air of night
　　　How they ring out their delight!—
　　　　From the molten-golden notes,
　　　　　　And all in tune,
　　　　What a liquid ditty floats
To the turtle-dove that listens, while she gloats
　　　　　On the moon!
　　　Oh, from out the sounding cells,
What a gush of euphony voluminously wells!
　　　　　　How it swells!
　　　　　　How it dwells
　　　　On the Future!—how it tells
　　　　Of the rapture that impels
　　　To the swinging and the ringing
　　　　Of the bells, bells, bells—
　　　Of the bells, bells, bells, bells,
　　　　　Bells, bells, bells—
To the rhyming and the chiming of the bells!

III

Hear the loud alarm bells—
Brazen bells!
What a tale of terror, now their turbulency tells!
In the startled ear of night
How they scream out their affright
Too much horrified to speak,
They can only shriek, shriek,
Out of tune,
In a clamorous appealing to the mercy of the fire,
In a mad expostulation with the deaf and frantic fire,
Leaping higher, higher, higher,
With a desperate desire,
And a resolute endeavor
Now—now to sit, or never
By the side of the pale-faced moon.
Oh, the bells, bells, bells!
What a tale their terror tells
Of Despair!
How they clang, and clash, and roar!
What a horror they outpour
On the bosom of the palpitating air!
Yet the ear, it fully knows,
By the twanging
And the clanging,
How the danger ebbs and flows;
Yet the ear distinctly tells,
In the jangling,
And the wrangling,
How the danger sinks and swells,
By the sinking or the swelling in the anger of the bells—
Of the bells—
Of the bells, bells, bells, bells,
Bells, bells, bells—
In the clamor and the clanging of the bells!

IV

Hear the tolling of the bells—
Iron bells!
What a world of solemn thought their monody compels!
In the silence of the night,
How we shiver with affright
At the melancholy menace of their tone!
For every sound that floats
From the rust within their throats
Is a groan.
And the people—ah, the people—
They that dwell up in the steeple,
All alone,
And who, tolling, tolling, tolling,
In that muffled monotone,
Feel a glory in so rolling
On the human heart a stone—
They are neither man nor woman—
They are neither brute nor human—
They are Ghouls:—
And their king it is who tolls:—
And he rolls, rolls, rolls,
Rolls
A paean from the bells;
And his merry bosom swells
With the paean of the bells!
And he dances, and he yells;
Keeping time, time, time,
In a sort of Runic rhyme,
To the paean of the bells:—
Of the bells:

Keeping time, time, time
In a sort of Runic rhyme,
    To the throbbing of the bells—
Of the bells, bells, bells—
    To the sobbing of the bells:—
Keeping time, time, time,
    As he knells, knells, knells,
In a happy Runic rhyme,
    To the rolling of the bells—
Of the bells, bells, bells—
    To the tolling of the bells—
Of the bells, bells, bells, bells,
        Bells, bells, bells—
To the moaning and the groaning of the bells.

Robert Browning
(1812-1889)

Robert Browning's characteristic vehicle for his best poetry is the so-called "dramatic monologue," in which a speaker-character reveals much about himself while he is talking ostensibly about someone else. "A Toccata of Galuppi's" is a good example of this genre. Because Browning's portraits are often psychological, his mode ironic, and his techniques experimental, he is a special favorite with modern poets and critics.

A TOCCATA OF GALUPPI'S

Oh Galuppi, Baldassare, this is very sad to find!
I can hardly misconceive you; it would prove me deaf and
    blind;
But although I take your meaning, 'tis with such a heavy
    mind!

Here you come with your old music, and here's all the good
    it brings.
What, they lived once thus at Venice where the merchants
    were the kings,
Where Saint Mark's is, where the Doges used to wed the
    sea with rings?

Ay, because the sea's the street there; and 'tis arched by. . .
    what you call
. . .Shylock's bridge with houses on it, where they kept the
    carnival:
I was never out of England—it's as if I saw it all.

Did young people take their pleasure when the sea was
    warm in May?
Balls and masks begun at midnight, burning ever to mid-
    day,
When they made up fresh adventures for the morrow, do
    you say?

Was a lady such a lady, cheeks so round and lips so red—
On her neck the small face buoyant, like a bellflower on its
    bed,
O'er the breast's superb abundance where a man might base
    his head?

Well, and it was graceful of them—they'd break talk off and afford
—She, to bite her mask's black velvet—he, to finger on his sword,
While you sat and played Toccatas, stately at the Clavichord?

What? Those lesser thirds so plaintive, sixths diminished, sigh on sigh,
Told them something? Those suspensions, those solutions —"Must we die?"
Those commiserating sevenths—"Life might last! we can but try!"

"Were you happy?" "Yes." "And are you still as happy?" "Yes. And you?"
"Then, more kisses!" "Did *I* stop them, when a million seemed so few?"
Hark, the dominant's persistence till it must be answered to!

So, an octave struck the answer. Oh, they praised you, I dare say!
"Brave Galuppi! that was music! good alike at grave and gay!
"I can always leave off talking when I hear a master play!"

Then they left you for their pleasure: till in due time, one by one,
Some with lives that came to nothing, some with deeds as well undone,
Death stepped tacitly and took them where they never see the sun.

But when I sit down to reason, think to take my stand nor
  swerve,
While I triumph o'er a secret wrung from nature's close
  · reserve,
In you come with your cold music till I creep through every
  nerve.

Yes, you, like a ghostly cricket, creaking where a house was
  burned:
"Dust and ashes, dead and done with, Venice spent what
  Venice earned.
"The soul, doubtless, is immortal—where a soul can be
  discerned.

"Yours for instance: you know physics, something of
  geology,
"Mathematics are your pastime; souls shall rise in their
  degree;
"Butterflies may dread extinction—you'll not die, it cannot
  be!

"As for Venice and her people, merely born to bloom and
  drop,
"Here on earth they bore their fruitage, mirth and folly
  were the crop:
"What of soul was left, I wonder, when the kissing had to
  stop?

"Dust and ashes!" So you creak it, and I want the heart to
  scold.
Dear dead women, with such hair, too—what's become of
  all the gold
Used to hang and brush their bosoms? I feel chilly and
  grown old.

Walt Whitman
(1819-1892)

A champion of the common man, democracy, and freedom, Walt Whitman is considered by some to be America's greatest and most influential national poet. Whitman's Leaves of Grass *underwent many revisions after its first publication in 1855. "Italian Music in Dakota" is contained in the edition of 1881. While the poet may have heard the "Seventeenth Regimental Band," he never actually visited "Dakota" (either one). He did, however, know his opera, as we can see from his references to Bellini's* La Sonnambula *and* Norma *and Donizetti's* Poliuto.

ITALIAN MUSIC IN DAKOTA
["The Seventeenth—the finest Regimental Band I ever heard."]

Through the soft evening air enwinding all,
Rocks, woods, fort, cannon, pacing sentries, endless wilds,
In dulcet streams, in flutes' and cornets' notes,
Electric, pensive, turbulent, artificial,
(Yet strangely fitting even here, meanings unknown before,
Subtler than ever, more harmony, as if born here, related
  here,
Not to the city's fresco'd rooms, not to the audience of the
  opera house,
Sounds, echoes, wandering strains, as really here at home,
Sonnambula's innocent love, trios with *Norma's* anguish,
And thy ecstatic chorus *Poliuto*;)
Ray'd in the limpid yellow slanting sundown,
Music, Italian music in Dakota.

While Nature, sovereign of this gnarl'd realm,
Lurking in hidden barbaric recesses,
Acknowledging rapport however far remov'd,
(As some old root or soil of earth its last-born flower or
  fruit,)
Listens well pleas'd.

~∽∽~

"Vincenzo Bellini" from a contemporary lithograph

Charles Baudelaire
(1821-1867)

Literary historians consider Charles Baudelaire the most influential French poet of the nineteenth century. Although his poetry is classical in form, the rich sensory images he used to establish symbolic correspondences represented a new technique and was much imitated. Baudelaire is credited with founding the Symbolist movement. His one volume, Les Fleurs du Mal *(The Flowers of Evil), was printed in a number of editions during the poet's lifetime. Baudelaire is also remembered for his translations of Edgar Allan Poe into French.*

MUSIC

translated by Lynne L. Gelber

Music often takes hold of me like a sea!
　　Towards my star so pale
Under a misty sky or into a vast ether
　　I set sail;

With chest extended and lungs filled out
　　Like sails,
I scramble up the back of banks of waves
　　Which the night veils;

I feel vibrating in me all the passions
　　Of a struggling vessel;
The soft wind, the storm and its convulsions

　　On the immense void
Cradle me. At other times, a flat calm, great mirror
　　Of my despair!

Thomas Hardy
(1840-1928)

Thomas Hardy is first thought of as a novelist, but his later career was centrally concerned with writing verse. Indeed, his reputation as a poet has been steadily increasing since his death. Hardy played the fiddle, and his fine poem "The Fiddler" treats the theme of the power of music.

THE FIDDLER

The fiddler knows what's brewing
    To the lilt of his lyric wiles:
The fiddler knows what rueing
    Will come of this night's smiles!

He sees couples join them for dancing,
    And afterwards joining for life,
He sees them pay high for their prancing
    By a welter of wedded strife.

He twangs: "Music hails from the devil,
    Though vaunted to come from heaven,
For it makes people do at a revel
    What multiplies sins by seven.

"There's many a heart now mangled,
    And waiting its time to go,
Whose tendrils were first entangled
    By my sweet viol and bow!"

"The Fiddler in the Inn" by Cornelis Dusart

67

William Butler Yeats
(1865-1939)

The lilt of William Butler Yeats' "The Fiddler of Dooney" captures something of the merry nature of the folk fiddler who will even find himself a dance to play for in heaven. Yeats was fascinated with Irish folk mythology and legend, and his poetry and poetic drama reflects his interest. Yeats won the 1923 Nobel Prize for Literature.

THE FIDDLER OF DOONEY

When I play on my fiddle in Dooney,
Folk dance like a wave of the sea;
My cousin is priest in Kilvarnet,
My brother in Moharabuiee.

I passed my brother and cousin:
They read in their books of prayer;
I read in my book of songs
I bought at the Sligo fair.

When we come at the end of time,
To Peter sitting in state,
He will smile on the three old spirits,
But call me first through the gate;

For the good are always the merry,
Save by an evil chance,
And the merry love the fiddle
And the merry love to dance:

And when the folk there spy me,
They will all come up to me,
With "Here is the fiddler of Dooney!"
And dance like a wave of the sea.

Edgar Lee Masters
(1869-1950)

In 1915 Edgar Lee Masters published Spoon River Anthology *anonymously, and it won him instant literary fame. The book contains a series of free verse portraits of the "secret lives" of now dead citizens of a fictional American small town. One such sketch concerned a certain "Fiddler Jones."*

FIDDLER JONES

The earth keeps some vibration going
There in your heart, and that is you.
And if the people find you can fiddle,
Why, fiddle you must, for all your life.
What do you see, a harvest of clover?
Or a meadow to walk through to the river?
The wind's in the corn; you rub your hands
For beeves hereafter ready for market;
Or else you hear the rustle of skirts
Like the girls when dancing at Little Grove.
To Cooney Potter a pillar of dust
Or whirling leaves meant ruinous drouth;
They looked to me like Red-Head Sammy
Stepping it off, to "Toor-a-Loor."
How could I till my forty acres
Not to speak of getting more,
With a medley of horns, bassoons and piccolos
Stirred in my brain by crows and robins
And the creak of a wind-mill—only these?
And I never started to plow in my life
That some one did not stop in the road
And take me away to a dance or picnic.
I ended up with forty acres;
I ended up with a broken fiddle—
And a broken laugh, and a thousand memories,
And not a single regret.

Courtesy of the National Gallery of Art, Washington, D.C.,
Chester Dale Collection

"The Old Musician" by Edouard Manet

Amy Lowell
(1874-1925)

Amy Lowell is remembered by some as the bulky, cigar-smoking woman from the famous Massachusetts family who wrote poems on dainty subjects like "Lilacs." Indeed, the poem "Music" presents a romantic flute player who "eats bread and onions," and by daylight "is fat and has a bald head." Lowell was very influential in stimulating interest in modern poetry and especially the Imagist movement.

MUSIC

The neighbour sits in his window and plays the flute,
From my bed I can hear him,
And the round notes flutter and tap about the room,
And hit against each other,
Blurring to unexpected chords.
It is very beautiful,
With the little flute-notes all about me,
In the darkness.

In the daytime,
The neighbour eats bread and onions with one hand
And copies music with the other.
He is fat and has a bald head,
So I do not look at him,
But run quickly past his window.
There is always the sky to look at,
Or the water in the well!

But when night comes and he plays his flute,
I think of him as a young man,
With gold seals hanging from his watch,
And a blue coat with silver buttons.
As I lie in my bed
The flute-notes push against my ears and lips,
And I go to sleep, dreaming.

"A Piece by Schumann" by Henri Fantin-Latour

Robert Frost
(1874-1963)

Robert Frost defies the easy categories that critics sometimes find convenient for grouping poets. He is curiously "old-fashioned" for a modern, too apparently easy and colloquial for a "serious" poet, too rooted in the New England landscape to speak universally. Genius is always difficult to pigeonhole. "The Aim Was Song" imagines man a music teacher instructing the wind in the ways of disciplined blowing.

THE AIM WAS SONG

Before man came to blow it right
  The wind once blew itself untaught,
And did its loudest day and night
  In any rough place where it caught.

Man came to tell it what was wrong:
  It hadn't found the place to blow;
It blew too hard—the aim was song.
  And listen—how it ought to go!

He took a little in his mouth,
  And held it long enough for north
To be converted into south,
  And then by measure blew it forth.

By measure. It was word and note,
  The wind the wind had meant to be—
A little through the lips and throat.
  The aim was song—the wind could see.

Rainer Maria Rilke
(1875-1926)

Rainer Maria Rilke's poetry is intensely lyrical, and characterized by striking visual imagery. Its feel is emotional, spiritual—even mystical. The poet's strong religious preoccupation and concern with death may account for this quality. "Piano Practice" captures an instant of emotion with intense vividness.

PIANO PRACTICE

translated by J. B. Leishman

The summer hums. The hot noon stupefies.
She breathed her fresh white dress distractedly,
and laid into the cogent exercise
impatience after some reality

might come to-morrow, or to-night—was there,
perhaps, already, though they kept it dark;
and then she all at once became aware,
through the tall windows, of the pampered park.

Thereupon stopped her playing; gazed out, clasped her
two hands together; longed for a long book—
and in a sudden fit of anger shook
the jasmin scent away. She found it rasped her.

Carl Sandburg
(1878-1967)

Influenced by Walt Whitman, Carl Sandburg's poetry seems indigenously American. Simple in diction and form, it is nonetheless powerful and memorable for the reader. Sandburg traveled the country at various times in his life singing native folksongs. As we can see from "Jazz Fantasia," the idiom of jazz fascinated him too.

JAZZ FANTASIA

Drum on your drums, batter on your banjoes,
sob on the long cool winding saxophones.
Go to it, O jazzmen.

Sling your knuckles on the bottoms of the happy tin pans,
let your trombones ooze, and go husha-husha-hush with
the slippery sand-paper.

Moan like an autumn wind high in the lonesome treetops,
   moan soft like
you wanted somebody terrible, cry like a racing car slipping
   away from a
motorcycle cop, bang-bang! you jazzmen, bang all together
   drums, traps,
banjoes, horns, tin cans—make two people fight on the top
   of a stairway
and scratch each other's eyes in a clinch tumbling down the
   stairs.

Can the rough stuff . . . now a Mississippi steamboat
   pushes up the night
river with a hoo-hoo-hoo-oo . . . and the green lanterns call-
   ing to the high
soft stars . . . a red moon rides on the humps of the low
   river hills . . .
go to it, O jazzmen.

"Jazz Trio" by Misch Kohn

85

Vachel Lindsay
(1879-1931)

Vachel Lindsay meant much of his poetry to be chanted, and his own performances initiated a vogue for public recitation during the early part of this century. Lindsay's verse attempts to capture a boisterous, exuberant, and noisy America. "The Flute of the Lonely" is written to the tune "Gaily the Troubadour."

THE FLUTE OF THE LONELY

Faintly the ne'er-do-well
Breathed through his flute:
All the tired neighbor-folk,
Hearing, were mute.
In their neat doorways sat,
Labors all done,
Helpless, relaxed, o'er-wrought,
Evening begun.

None of them there beguiled
Work-thoughts away,
Like to this reckless, wild
Loafer by day.
(Weeds in his flowers upgrown!
Fences awry!
Rubbish and bottles heaped!
Yard like a sty!)

There in his lonely door,
Leering and lean,
Staggering, liquor-stained,
Outlawed, obscene—
Played he his moonlight thought,
Mastered his flute.
All the tired neighbor-folk,
Hearing, were mute.
None but he, in that block,
Knew such a tune.
All loved the strain, and all
Looked at the moon!

Courtesy of the Prints Division, New York Public Library, Astor, Lenox and Tilden Foundation

"The Flute" by Felix Vallotton

89

Wallace Stevens
(1879-1955)

Wallace Stevens, for much of his working life an insurance company executive, is recognized now as one of America's truly outstanding poets. A master at creating fictive landscapes, his verse attempted to structure the natural chaos he found everywhere. Some of his poem titles point to his musical interest: "Peter Quince at the Clavier," "Mozart, 1935," "The Man with the Blue Guitar," "Asides on the Oboe," and "Piano Practice at the Academy of the Holy Angels."

PIANO PRACTICE AT THE ACADEMY OF THE HOLY ANGELS

The time will come for these children, seated before their
long black instruments, to strike the themes of love—
All of them, darkened by time, moved by they know not
what, amending the airs they play to fulfill themselves;
Seated before these shining forms, like the duskiest glass,
reflecting the piebald of roses or what you will.
Blanche, the blonde, whose eyes are not wholly straight, in
a room of lustres, shed by turquoise falling,
Whose heart will murmur with the music that will be a
voice for her, speaking the dreaded change of speech;
And Rosa, the muslin dreamer of satin and cowry-kin, dis-
daining the empty keys; and the young infanta,
Jocunda, who will arrange the roses and rearrange, letting
the leaves lie on the water-like lacquer;
And that confident one, Marie, the wearer of cheap stones,
who will have grown still and restless;
And Crispine, the blade, reddened by some touch, demand-
ing the most from the phrases
Of the well-thumbed, infinite pages of her masters, who
will seem old to her, requiting less and less her feeling:
In the days when the mood of love will be swarming for
solace and sink deeply into the thin stuff of being,
And these long, black instruments will be so little to them
that will be needing so much, seeking so much in their
music.

William Carlos Williams
(1883-1963)

America's most famous physician-poet, William Carlos Williams once wrote the libretto for an opera based on George Washington's life. But it is for his carefully observed imagistic poetry that he is celebrated. In "The Dance," Williams "translates" the vital and energetic swirl of dancing bodies in Brueghel's painting into exuberant rhythmic language.

THE DANCE

In Brueghel's great picture, The Kermess,
the dancers go round, they go round and
around, the squeal and the blare and the
tweedle of bagpipes, a bugle and fiddles
tipping their bellies (round as the thick-
sided glasses whose wash they impound)
their hips and their bellies off balance
to turn them. Kicking and rolling about
the Fair Grounds, swinging their butts, those
shanks must be sound to bear up under such
rollicking measures, prance as they dance
in Brueghel's great picture, The Kermess

"The Wedding Dance" by Pieter Brueghel the Elder

D. H. Lawrence
(1885-1930)

D. H. Lawrence is best known for such notorious novels as Sons and Lovers *and* Lady Chatterley's Lover. *Too few know him as a fine poet and, indeed, it was his poetry that first gained Lawrence critical attention. In "Piano" we have a speaker nostalgically remembering his childhood days and longing for them again.*

PIANO

Softly, in the dusk, a woman is singing to me;
Taking me back down the vista of years, till I see
A child sitting under the piano, in the boom of the tingling
    strings
And pressing the small, poised feet of a mother who smiles
    as she sings.

In spite of myself, the insidious master of song
Betrays me back, till the heart of me weeps to belong
To the old Sunday evenings at home, with winter outside
And hymns in the cozy parlor, the tinkling piano our guide.

So now it is vain for the singer to burst into clamor
With the great black piano appassionato. The glamour
Of childish days is upon me, my manhood is cast
Down in the flood of remembrance, I weep like a child for
    the past.

Conrad Aiken
(1889-1973)

Influenced by Walter Pater's idea that one art can learn from another, Conrad Aiken took music as tutor for his poetry. Consequently, Aiken's verse is much concerned with attempts to render the sounds, structures, and feel of music in language. The poem reprinted here demonstrates Aiken's success. We can almost hear his oboe and flute.

MUSIC

The calyx of the oboe breaks,
silver and soft the flower it makes.
And next, beyond, the flute-notes seen
now are white and now are green.

What are these sounds, what daft device,
mocking at flame, mimicking ice?
Musicians, will you never rest
from strange translations of the breast?

The heart, from which all horrors come,
grows like a vine, its gourd a drum;
the living pattern sprawls and climbs
eager to bear all worlds and times:
trilling leaf and tinkling grass
glide into darkness clear as glass;
then the musicians cease to play
and the world is waved away.

Edna St. Vincent Millay
(1892-1950)

One of Edna St. Vincent Millay's treasured experiences was hearing Enrico Caruso in Aïda *at the Metropolitan Opera. The poet's interest in opera resulted in her libretto for* The King's Henchmen *by Deems Taylor. It is for her sonnets, however, that Millay is especially remembered. "On Hearing a Symphony of Beethoven" is written in the English or Shakespearean sonnet form, with three quatrains and a couplet at the end.*

101

ON HEARING A SYMPHONY
OF BEETHOVEN

Sweet sounds, oh, beautiful music, do not cease!
Reject me not into the world again.
With you alone is excellence and peace,
Mankind made plausible, his purpose plain.
Enchanted in your air benign and shrewd,
With limbs a-sprawl and empty faces pale,
The spiteful and the stingy and the rude
Sleep like the scullions in the fairy-tale.
This moment is the best the world can give:
The tranquil blossom on the tortured stem.
Reject me not, sweet sounds! oh, let me live,
Till Doom espy my towers and scatter them,
A city spell-bound under the aging sun,
Music my rampart, and my only one.

"Beethoven," etching from lithograph by Kriehuber

E. E. Cummings
(1894-1962)

Modern music and art clearly influenced E. E. Cummings'
poetry. It is remarkable for its eccentricities of typography,
punctuation, use of language, etc. At his best Cummings in-
tegrated form and content to produce memorable verse. Though
not modern, the Luca della Robbia carving seems to illustrate
"These Children Singing in Stone a" perfectly.

THESE CHILDREN SINGING
IN STONE A

these children singing in stone a
silence of stone these
little children wound with stone
flowers opening for

ever these silently lit
the children are petals
their song is a flower of
always their flowers

of stone are
silently singing
a song more silent
than silence these always

children forever
singing wreathed with singing
blossoms children of
stone with blossoming

eyes
know if a
lit tle
tree listens

forever to always children singing forever
a song made
of silent as stone silence of
song

Choir Panel by Luca della Robbia

Babette Deutsch
(1895-1982)

Internationally recognized poet and critic, Babette Deutsch is perhaps best known for her study Poetry in Our Time. *Her "Piano Recital" is inscribed for pianist Maro Ajemian and composer John Cage. It presents a vivid poetic picture of a musician's swan-like grace and strength of performance.*

PIANO RECITAL

Her drooping wrist, her arm
Move as a swan should move,
First singing when death dawns
Upon the plumaged flesh.
But here no swan wings thresh
No river runs. A woman
Strikes hidden strings in love.

Now slow—as fronds of palms—
Her fingers on the keys.
Lifted, her listening arms
Ponder the theme afresh.
Until it seems young flesh
Is momently transmured
To echo's effigy.

No no—the risen hands
Pounce on the keys, destroy
The hush, rush on, command
The blacks, the ivories,
In fight now with the keys
To grief's unwindowed prison.
To the low gate of joy.

She leans with sparkling looks
Toward the dark wood, her strong
Hands work as gleamers should.
Then, as who would caress
A birdlike wordlessness,
She stoops—to drink the meaning
At the still brink of song.

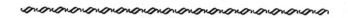

Louise Bogan
(1897-1970)

Louise Bogan's verse is often suggestive of seventeenth-century metaphysical poetry because of its concentrated diction and imagery. The "Musician" of her poem reprinted here seems to be a harpist, whose hands are as necessary to the strings of the instrument as those strings are to the performer's hands.

MUSICIAN

Where have these hands been,
By what delayed,
That so long stayed
Apart from the thin

Strings which they now grace
With their lonely skill?
Music and their cool will
At last interlace.

Now with great ease, and slow,
The thumb, the finger, the strong
Delicate hand plucks the long
String it was born to know.

And, under the palm, the string
Sings as it wished to sing.

∽∽

Courtesy of the Prints Division, New York Public Library,
Astor, Lenox and Tilden Foundation

"Harp Player" by Emanuele Romano

Langston Hughes
(1902-1967)

Discovered by poet Vachel Lindsay, who helped get his first volume of verse published, Langston Hughes is one of the most celebrated modern Black writers. He used the music of the '20s—jazz, blues, even the Cuban rumba—for poetic inspiration. His language makes use of Black dialects. As we can see in "African Dance," Hughes was ever conscious of his roots.

AFRICAN DANCE

The low beating of the tom-toms,
The slow beating of the tom-toms,
　　Low . . . slow
　　Slow . . . low—
Stirs your blood.

　　　Dance!
A night-veiled girl
　　Whirls softly into a
　　Circle of light.
　　Whirls softly . . . slowly,
Like a wisp of smoke around the fire—
　　And the tom-toms beat,
　　And the tom-toms beat,
And the low beating of the tom-toms
　　Stirs your blood.

"Head of a Negro" by Peter Paul Rubens 117

W. H. Auden
(1907-1973)

The Anglo-American poet W. H. Auden became interested in music when young. While in school he learned to play the piano, and won several prizes for his musical achievement. Later in life he became friends with composer Igor Stravinsky, for whom he co-authored the libretto to The Rake's Progress. *He also had a hand in a new version of Mozart's* The Magic Flute. *"The Composer" suggests that the writing of music is the purest act of creation.*

THE COMPOSER

All the others translate: the painter sketches
A visible world to love or reject;
Rummaging into his living, the poet fetches
The images out that hurt and connect,

From Life to Art by painstaking adaption,
Relying on us to cover the rift;
Only your notes are pure contraption,
Only your song is an absolute gift.

Pour out your presence, a delight cascading
The falls of the knee and the weirs of the spine,
Our climate of silence and doubt invading;

You alone, alone, imaginary song,
Are unable to say an existence is wrong,
And pour out your forgiveness like a wine.

"Beethoven in His Study" by Karl Scholesser

Gwendolyn Brooks
(1917-   )

Gwendolyn Brooks is perhaps the preeminent living Black poet. Born in Topeka, Kansas and raised in Chicago, she began writing seriously in 1941. She won the 1950 Pulitzer Prize for her volume Annie Allen. *She is poet laureate of the state of Illinois, having succeeded Carl Sandburg in this capacity. "Piano After War" is a conventional sonnet, but is distinguished by subtle rhyming and an arresting statement.*

PIANO AFTER WAR

On a snug evening I shall watch her fingers,
Cleverly ringed, declining to clever pink,
Beg glory from the willing keys. Old hungers
Will break their coffins, rise to eat and thank.
And music, warily, like the golden rose
That sometimes after sunset warms the west,
Will warm that room, persuasively suffuse
That room and me, rejuvenate a past.
But suddenly, across my climbing fever
Of proud delight—a multiplying cry.
A cry of bitter dead men who will never
Attend a gentle maker of musical joy.
Then my thawed eye will go again to ice.
And stone will shove the softness from my face.

Barry Targan
(1932-   )

Barry Targan's poetry and fiction has appeared widely in the best popular and "little" magazines and in a number of collections. He teaches creative writing at the State University of New York at Binghamton. The poem "Music at the Last" was written during a time of violin study with the editor of this book.

MUSIC AT THE LAST

I play the violin
like Bach composed
for choruses
that he would never hear.
I reach for high positions
that I find like Beethoven
in the inner ear
found music.
Music at the last.

My fingers fail.

Bright Will is unequivalent
to the dream:

audacity of arpeggios,
bold leapers along
strict, shattering edges,
triple stops mounting up
and up into incalculable sums,
the arrows of harmonies on the E.

My fingers fail.

But music comes to live
upon the chords of mind
where music at the last
is bound no more
and will not dim.

"Violinist" by Charles C. Curran

About the Author

Dr. Murray J. Levith is Professor of English at Skidmore College where he teaches Shakespeare and Renaissance Literature. Professor Levith is also a violinist, having played professionally in several symphony orchestras. He has authored a number of books including *Renaissance and Modern* (1976), *What's in Shakespeare's Names* (1978), *Fiddlers in Fiction* (1979), and *Musical Masterpieces in Prose* (1981). He lives with his wife and two sons in Saratoga Springs, New York.